The Manager's Book of Questions

The Manager's Book of Questions

751

Great Interview Questions for Hiring the Best Person

John Kador

McGraw-Hill

New York   San Francisco   Washington, D.C.   Auckland   Bogotá
Caracas   Lisbon   London   Madrid   Mexico City   Milan
Montreal   New Delhi   San Juan   Singapore
Sydney   Tokyo   Toronto

McGraw-Hill

*A Division of The **McGraw·Hill** Companies*

8 9 0   DOC/DOC   0 2 1 0

ISBN 0-07-034311-X

The sponsoring editor for this book was Betsy Brown, the editing supervisor was Penny Linskey, and the production supervisor was Pamela Pelton. It was set in Sabon by Priscilla Beer of McGraw-Hill's Professional Book Group composition unit.

Printed and bound by R. R. Donnelley and Sons Company.

McGraw-Hill books are available at special quantity discounts to use as premiums and sales promotions, or for use in corporate training programs. For more information, please write to the Director of Special Sales, McGraw-Hill, Professional Publishing, Two Penn Plaza, New York, NY 10121-2298. Or contact your local bookstore.

 This book is printed on recycled, acid-free paper containing a minimum of 50% recycled, de-inked fiber.

For Anna Beth, Danny, and Rachel
Without Question

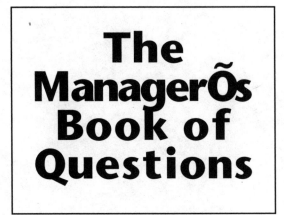

The Manager's Book of Questions

Contents

Top 10 Toughest Questions 81

IntroductionÑ Interviewing Is Serious Business

Have you ever faced a stack of résumés and wondered just how you would be able to identify the best candidate for a job? If you've ever been at a loss for what to ask in an upcoming interview, now you'll be able to pull out this handy quick reference tool and find the best questions to ask in each and every interview. The interview process is designed to answer three basic questions:

- Does the candidate have the skills or experience to do the job?
- Does the candidate want the job?
- Will the candidate fit in?

All the questions in this book speak to one of these three concerns. If you stick to the listed questions and apply them consistently and professionally across interviews, there can be no basis for charges of discrimination or bias.

How This Book Is Organized

The questions in this book are organized by function and skill sets. For example, ice-breaking questions can be found in Chapter 1 (Getting Things Started). General background questions are in Chapter 5 (So Tell Me About Yourself). To judge whether a candidate is experienced in such areas as administration, finance, sales management, customer service, project management, or information technology, see Chapter 10 (Assessing Specific Skill Sets). Money questions are addressed in Chapter 9. Questions for closing the interview are in Chapter 12.

With workplace violence at an all-time high, anything a company can do to screen out disgruntled or potentially violent candidates becomes critical. See Chapter 12 (Do You Have a Problem with That?) for a list of questions that may help identify candidates with histories or inclinations toward violence.

A job interview has just begun when the interviewer has finished asking questions. Now it's the candidate's turn to ask questions. The interviewer must be prepared to answer these questions as accurately and completely as possible. Fortunately, experience has shown that the types of questions candidates can be expected to ask are fairly predictable. Chapter 13 (Now, Do You Have Any Questions?) offers interviewers an opportunity to prepare for these queries.

What Personal Questions Are Acceptable?

What personal questions are you entitled to ask a candidate? While advice on this critical issue is beyond the scope of this book, Appendix D includes a discussion of the principles of asking fair and effective questions as well as a list of acceptable personal questions. Appendix E lists a number of unacceptable personal questions to avoid at all costs. The bottom line? If you can't make an obvious case for why the question is related to the job at hand, avoid asking it.

For example, it's unacceptable to ask a candidate if he or she has any disabilities. However, if the job requires the ability to lift up to 50 packages per day, each of which weighs up to 30 pounds, you can ask each applicant you interview: "This job requires the ability to lift up to fifty 30-pound packages per day. Would this requirement be a problem for you?"

Just be sure to ask everyone the same question in the same way. Similarly, you can't ask if an applicant's responsibility for small children will keep them from meeting the job's travel requirements. You can, however, ask each applicant something like this: "As you know, the job involves 30 percent overnight travel, often on short notice. Would this be a problem for you?"

The bottom line is that the question must be job-related and asked of each applicant in the same way.

Favorite Questions of Top Recruiters

Do you have a favorite interviewing question? If you are like most experienced interviewers, you find that you ask the same question of virtually every person you are interviewing. There is something about the question that gives you important insights about the candidate and the more you use it the more powerful it seems. This book gives you an opportunity to read the favorite interviewing questions of some of your counterparts. Peppered throughout the book are the favorite questions of senior human resource executives at Fortune 500 organizations.

Included with the questions are the executives' ruminations about what kinds of responses they look for.

Asking Questions Is Good: Listening Is Better

A set of good questions—even great ones—does not a good interview make. A good interview is a function of the interviewer's capacity for listening, for paying attention, for maintaining an attitude of complete respect. The most effective interviewers act on the basis that it is a privilege to ask questions and an honor to listen to another human being.

Nevertheless, all things being equal, the questions in this book can make the process of hiring the right person for your job or team more effective. Many of the questions in the book are new in content or wording. Asking questions a candidate has not considered before minimizes the role-playing quality of many interviews. Any question that requires a candidate to do original thinking gives interviewers a chance to assess how he or she thinks and communicates.

Still, there is no substitute for listening and lots of time. Theoretically, an interviewer with world-class listening skills and a couple of hours should be able to get by with a single question, the so-called "killer" question: "So, tell me a little about yourself." Complemented by appropriate follow-up probes and a lot of time, a good listener using this one question should be able to get everything he or she needs to make a sound decision.

One problem is that most candidates have rehearsed their answers to this popular question. The result is a higher level of pretense than desirable. Another problem is that the interviewer's attention span and total time available to interviewers must be divided among multiple candidates. *751 Questions* solves this problem by offering perceptive questions that will elicit the frank unrehearsed answers you as a manager are looking for.

Questions Yes; Answers No

Don't look in these pages for answers to any of the questions listed. Few of the questions have responses that can be deemed right or wrong, correct or incorrect. The questions are better regarded as jumping off points for the interviewer to listen carefully—with one's eyes as well as ears—and ask pointed follow-up questions: "Why? Can you give me an example? Is that what you still think?"

Keep an open mind. The specific content of the answer is rarely the key element you should be listening for. Resist the temptation to favor a candidate whose answer happens to agree with your own. Observe body language. Pay attention not only to what is being said but to how it is being said. Does the person maintain eye contact? Does his or her voice drop with insecurity? Does he or she fidget? Does the person project confidence? Is there a level of enthusiasm? These attributes of a candidate speak just as loudly as content.

Be Consistent and Take Notes

The best defense against a charge of discrimination or bias is to consistently ask nondiscriminatory questions. When interviewing, make sure you ask the same set of questions in a similar manner.

Finally, write the questions down, leaving room to make notes. Documenting all the interviews protects you in a variety of ways. Make sure, however, to note only objective facts—dates, skills, education, etc. Stay away from impressions or physical descriptions. These notes will be necessary to refer to when you make a hiring decision. Then, just to be safe, retain those notes for a minimum of a year, or whatever amount of time exceeds the statute of limitations for filing discrimination claims in your state.

How to Use This Book

This book gives managers and team builders the precise questions they need to screen and select applicants for a job or team. It is designed to lead you to the questions appropriate for an upcoming interview. Organized around the typical interview process, the book opens with ice-breaking questions and progresses through the various stages of the typical interview.

A good way to start organizing a set of interview questions is to get a handful of blank index cards. As you go through the book, select questions for the interview by copying them on individual index cards. A typical 45-minute interview has time for an average of 15 questions, so be judicious. Pick only the questions that you believe are most pertinent. If you end up with 20 to 25 cards, you will have the raw material to fine-tune a focused interview.

After you have listed the questions on index cards (or on a computer database or word processing file) you need to arrange them in order from opening to closing. Many interviews flow better when the questions go from the general to the specific. Try to front-load the interview with the easier, less threatening questions. Save the questions about money for the end.

For anyone who is faced with hiring staff, *751 Questions* is an indispensable tool for making the best hiring decisions.

John Kador

Acknowledgments

At the same time that I am grateful to all the people who have helped make this book a reality, I recognize the impossibility of thanking them all.

Most of the people to whom I'm grateful didn't realize they were helping me. I'm not proud to admit that in a lifetime of collecting questions much like other people collect quotations, couplets, or epigraphs, I conspicuously failed to make note of the sources.

Nevertheless, thanks go to all the teachers, professors, job interviewers, reporters, columnists, and acquaintances from every corner of my life who have challenged me over the years with questions great and small. They rarely received the answers they were seeking, so perhaps they will find a small measure of comfort in knowing that I at least remembered the questions.

More recently I have kept track of my obligations. Here's a tip of the hat to all the human resources executives who gave me the benefit of their interviewing experience: Barbara Brannon, John Bono, Gary Clark, Alan M. Forker, Gordon Housworth, Elizabeth Loker, Candace Mendenhall, Tom Morgan, Tony Rucci, Fran Sincere, Paul Slattery, David Swan. I have nothing but admiration for the many people who took time out of their hectic days to answer my many questions as I was writing this book: Bob Gately, Donald Gentry, Anne C. Gingras, Kirby Glad, Tim Hicks, Clyde C. Lowstuter, Lindsey Novak, John Sifonis, and Irv N. Zukerman. I am indebted to Bob Thomas, the former publisher of *Enterprise Systems Journal*, for first encouraging me to think about questions.

I appreciate Rita Hoover, whose careful reading of the manuscript flagged a number of questionable items. Thanks go also to my many other friends at Extended Partners who encouraged me and never questioned this project even when I did: Mark Allen, Laura Crites, Laura Hill, George Moskoff, Steve Vasilion, and Loy Williams.

Finally, for Danny's and Rachel's expressions of pride in me and this book, I am endlessly grateful.

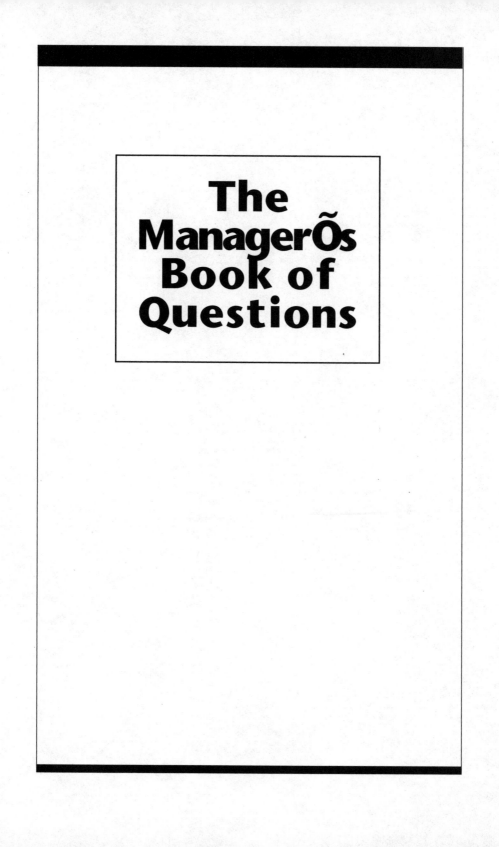

The Manager's Book of Questions

CHAPTER
1

GETTING THINGS STARTED
25 Questions to Get the Ball Rolling

The purpose of a job interview is for the interviewer and the job candidate to get to know one another.

A job interview is an inherently stressful experience. The business of two people getting to know each other is never enhanced by anxiety, so the first order of business is for the interviewer to establish rapport and put the candidate at ease. As an interviewer, that's your first responsibility. The first few minutes are also the hardest part of any interview.

Your job as interviewer is simple: You control the *flow* of the interview and its tone. For the most part, the applicant controls the content, because, after all, he or she decides how to answer your questions. But the order of the interview and its formality are your choice.

The easiest way to establish rapport and set the tone of the interview is to call the candidate by name. The culture of your organization will dictate whether you elect to call the candidate by the candidate's first name or surname. Ask yourself, "Do I call my supervisor 'Charlie' or 'Mr. Smith'?" If the accepted practice at your company is to use first names to address superiors, then by all means use the candidate's first name during the interview. Encourage the use of your first name. Use the candidate's first name often. Most people appreciate people who remember and use their names and they will be put at ease by the gesture. At the same time, you will be subtly communicating something about the style and culture of your organization.

Create a pleasant environment for the interview, since a relaxed candidate will tend to give you more complete and authentic information.

A point about note-taking: If you are going to take notes, it is often useful to say a word about why you are doing so. "Richard, I hope you don't mind my taking notes. It's the best way I know to make sure I won't forget the important matters we are discussing today." Many people are intimidated by having their utterances recorded, so be as up front and relaxed about what you are doing as possible.

The initial questions you ask will determine the success of the interview. The general principle is to start with general issues that relate to the reason both of you are meeting: the job interview itself. It's best to avoid substantial, specific questions about the candidate or the requirements of the job. There will be plenty of time for that. Right now, you want to get some housekeeping details out of the way. The first order of business is to welcome the candidate and thank him or her for coming. After you have reviewed the requirements of the job you are trying to fill and the candidate's résumé or application, you can begin to get a general picture of the candidate.

1. Did you have any trouble finding us?

2. How do you know about this job and organization?

3. What kind of work do you want to do?

4. How would your friends describe you? Your professors?

5. What else should I know about you?

6. What are your expectations of your future employer?

7. What two or three things are important to you in your new position.

8. What goals have you set for yourself and how are you planning to achieve them?

9. Who has had the greatest influence on the development of your career interests?

10. Would your supervisor be surprised to learn that you are seeking new employment?

11. How long have you been looking for a job?

12. Why do you want to leave your current position?

13. Have you received any offers so far?

14. How far can you advance with your current employer?

15. If you are so happy where you are, why are you looking for another job?

16. Do you know much about our company, department, team?

17. Why would you like to work for us?

18. How does this job compare with others you've applied for?

19. What is the ideal position for you in any company?

20. Based on what you know about our industry right now, how does your ideal job stack up against the description of the job you're applying for?

21. If you could make a wish, what would be your perfect job?

22. What causes you to lose your temper?

23. What two adjectives best describe you?

24. What are your best professional skills?

25. If you were in my position, would you hire you?

CHAPTER
2

WHAT HAVE YOU DONE UP TILL NOW?

50 Questions on the Candidate's Work History

The single best predictor of success in one assignment is the applicant's performance at his or her last assignment.

This truism is the basis for most job interviews. Interviews that probe for past job behavior as an insight into future job behavior have been found to be most reliable. The most successful human resource managers agree that the way in which an applicant handled a specific situation in the past gives the best indication of how he or she will approach a similar situation in the future. If an applicant has been able to adapt to change quickly in the past, he or she most likely will be comfortable with change in the future. If an applicant has demonstrated a good track record in sales, you can predict that he or she will continue to be an effective salesperson in the future.

This is the basis of behavior-based interviewing. As the interviewer, you have the challenge to understand the requirements of the new position and to present the applicant with questions that will reveal his or her past functioning in specific areas.

1. In your capacity as a _____ at _____ company, what did you actually do? Please provide details.

2. What do you feel are the biggest challenges facing this field? This industry?

3. Tell me about your last (or present) job.

4. What do you think it takes for a person to be successful in your particular area?

5. How long have you been looking for a position?

6. How have previous jobs equipped you for greater responsibility?

7. What aspects of your current job would you consider to be crucial to the success of the business? Why?

8. What was the least relevant job you have held?

9. How long will it take for you to make a contribution?

10. What did (or do) you enjoy most about your last (or present) job?

11. What did (or do) you enjoy least about your last (or present) job?

12. What were (or are) the biggest pressures on your last (or present) job?

13. Have you held other positions like the one you are applying for today? If yes, describe how you expect the positions to be the same.

14. In what ways do you expect them to differ?

15. What is the most important thing you learned from your previous experience that you will bring to this job?

16. If there were two things you could change in your last (or present) job, what would they be and how would you change them?

17. Why did you leave your last job? (or: Why do you want to leave your present job?)

18. Why do you think you were successful in your last job?

19. How has your last (or present) job changed since you've held it?

20. Please describe your last (or present) supervisor's management style.

21. If you could make one constructive suggestion to your last (or present) CEO, what would it be?

22. Of all the work you have done, where have you been the most successful?

23. Describe to me how your job relates to the overall goals of your department and company.

24. What are the most repetitive tasks in your job?

25. To what extent have you automated your last job?

26. What technical decisions did you have to make?

27. What decisions or judgment calls did you have to make in these areas?

28. What were the most important projects you worked on at your last job?

29. Can you give a ratio for the amount of time you worked alone to the amount of time you worked with others?

30. How effectively did your boss handle evaluations?

31. Tell me about a method you've developed to accomplish a job. What were its strengths and weaknesses?

32. How many hours a week, on the average, do you find it necessary to work to get your job done?

33. Can you describe a situation where a crisis occurred and you had to shift priorities and workload quickly?

34. How do you feel about your present workload?

35. In what ways has your manager contributed to your choosing to leave your present job?

36. How do you think your supervisor will react when you tender your resignation?

37. Describe the most significant report or presentation you had to prepare.

38. What idea have you developed and implemented that was particularly creative or innovative?

39. Take me through a project where you demonstrated _____ skills.

40. Tell me about a team project of which you are particularly proud and your specific contribution.

41. Tell me about a difficult decision you had to make.

42. What made it difficult? What did you learn?

43. Describe the way your department is currently organized.

44. What was the hardest decision you ever had to make, and how did you handle it?

45. What are the most difficult aspects of your current job, and how do you approach them?

46. What has been your most important work-related innovation or contribution?

47. What caused you the most problems in executing your tasks?

48. How do you organize and plan for major projects? Recall for me a major project you worked on. How did you organize and plan for it?

49. What would you say are some of the basic factors that motivate you in your work?

50. You've had little experience in _____ . How do you intend to learn what you need to know to perform well in this job?

CHAPTER 3

WHAT DO YOU BRING TO THE TABLE?
100 Questions to Determine Fit

Most employers hire on competence and fire on job fit.

Employers need their employees to have specific skill sets because they need specific tasks accomplished. One of the main challenges of any screening process is to ensure that applicants are minimally qualified to meet the challenges of the position for which they are applying. Concern about a candidate's abilities is obvious. Fortunately, verifying abilities is not too difficult, especially when the skills can be easily tested. Reference checks represent another way claims of expertise can be verified. But the job interview is a first-line process to determine whether the candidate truly has the minimal skills required to succeed in the job.

Chapter 10 lists questions to determine levels of preparedness in such specific areas as finance and administration, sales and marketing, and information technology. This chapter offers more general questions to determine an applicant's ability to function in your organization. These questions are designed to show that the candidate will fit into the work environment. Included in this chapter is a list of questions that begin: "Tell me about a time when you ..." Many interviewers find questions phrased in this way to be particularly powerful.

1. Please take me through your professional career.

2. Why have you chosen this particular field?

3. What aspects of your education (or job) do you rate as most critical?

4. What would your greatest business *champion* say about you?

5. What would your greatest business *adversary* say about you?

6. What are your long-range goals?

7. If we hired you, what are the top three goals you would like to see this company (department, team) achieve?

8. What can you do for us that someone else cannot?

9. Have you done your best work yet?

10. What do you like most about this job?

11. What aspect of this job is the least appealing?

12. How do you plan your time?

13. What are three reasons for your success?

14. What kind of leader are you? Please provide an example.

15. What is the title of the person you report to and what are his or her responsibilities?

16. Think back to a time when you trained a new employee. Tell me exactly what you did to train that employee and bring the person up to the job's performance standards.

17. What were the biggest decisions you made in the past six months?

18. How did you go about making them and what alternatives did you consider?

19. Can you describe a major project with which you encountered problems?

20. How did you resolve them and what were the results?

21. Describe one of the best ideas you have ever sold to a peer or supervisor. What were your approach and result?

22. What kinds of obstacles to completing assignments on time do you most frequently encounter at work?

23. What strategies have you devised to handle such obstacles?

24. How do you know you are doing a good job?

25. How do you prefer to measure performance?

26. Can you recall a time when you were less than pleased with your performance?

27. Can you describe some projects that were a result of your own initiative?

28. What prompted you to begin such projects? How did they end up?

29. What qualifications do you have to make you successful in this field?

30. Do you prefer to speak with someone or send a memo?

31. How do you motivate people?

32. Give an example of a situation in which you failed, and how you handled it.

33. What characteristics are the most important in a good manager? How have you displayed these characteristics?

34. What two or three accomplishments have given you the most satisfaction?

35. Describe a leadership role of yours and tell me why you committed your time to it.

36. Have you been in charge of budgeting, approving expenses, and monitoring departmental progress against financial goals?

37. What suggestions did you make in your last job to cut costs, increase profits, improve morale, increase output, etc.?

38. What results did you get? How do you know? How did you measure results?

39. What would you like to have done more of in your last job?

40. What specific strengths did you bring to your last job?

41. What would you consider the three most significant accomplishments in your business life?

42. Think of something that you consider a failure in your career. What did you learn from it?

43. Can you think of an example of a lesson you learned from someone else's mistake?

44. What risks did you take in your last few jobs? What was the result of those risks?

45. What languages do you speak?

46. What do you think differentiates you from the other applicants for this job? Why?

47. Why do you think you'd be a good fit for this job?

48. What do you do when you are having trouble solving a problem?

49. What interests you most about this position?

50. Have you ever hired anyone?

51. On what basis do you select a new hire?

52. Describe the people that you hired on your last job. Did they work out? How long did they remain at their jobs?

53. Have you ever fired anyone? On what basis did you fire them?

54. How would you describe your management philosophy?

55. What kind of references do you think your previous employer will give you? Why?

56. If you have complaints about your present employers, and they think so highly of you, why haven't you brought your concerns to their attention?

57. The successful candidate for this position will be working with some highly trained individuals who have been with the company for a long time. How will you fit in with them?

58. What is the most difficult situation you have faced? How did you handle it?

59. How did your supervisor get the best performance out of you?

60. How do you use deadlines in your work?

61. How would you do this job differently from other people?

62. What personality traits do you think are necessary to succeed in this field?

63. Have you thought about why you might prefer to work with our firm as opposed to one of the other firms to which you've applied?

64. When some managers make a decision, they often feel a need to defend it. Can you describe a time when you changed a stated decision or opinion because you were persuaded you were wrong?

65. What would you do differently in your life? Your career?

66. If you could eliminate one responsibility from your last job, what would it be?

(Questions for Applicants with Long Tenure at One Company.)

67. After being with the same company for so long, do you think it will be hard to adapt to a new organization?

68. Some people feel that spending so much time at one job demonstrates a lack of initiative. How do you respond to that?

69. What are the advantages of staying at one job a long time?

70. Since you were in the same job for such a long time, you've probably grown very comfortable in it—maybe even a bit stale. How would you cope with a new job in a company such as ours?

(Questions for Job Hoppers.)

71. You've changed jobs quite frequently. How do we know you'll stick around if we hire you?

72. How do you explain the diversity of jobs you've had? The positions don't seem to be in a logical progression.

73. You've been with your current employer for only a short amount of time. Is this an indication that you'll be moving around a lot throughout your career?

74. How long will you stay here at this company?

75. What strategies have you found to be successful in managing unfair criticism?

76. Can you describe a time when you pushed too hard for a project to the detriment of the project?

77. Give me some examples of different approaches you have used when persuading someone to cooperate with you.

78. How do you cope with the inevitable stresses and pressures of any job?

TELL ME ABOUT A TIME WHEN YOU ...

For some candidates, a set of questions beginning with the words "Tell me about a time when you..." may be particularly revealing.

This formulation is a variety of an open-ended question that makes some candidates feel more comfortable with sharing specific information. For example, some applicants find themselves less defensive responding to "Tell me about a time when you made a mistake" as opposed to the more aggressive "Have you ever made a mistake?" The latter is accusatory, while the former seems to offer applicants permission to share an experience. The interviewer may consider adding a few questions of this form to the interview template.

Tell me about a time when you ...

79. Worked effectively under pressure.

80. Handled a difficult situation with a coworker.

81. Were creative in solving a problem.

82. Were unable to complete a project on time.

83. Persuaded team members to do things your way.

84. Had to take a stand on an

unpopular position.

85. Wrote a program (or report or strategic plan) that was well received.

86. Anticipated potential problems and developed a proactive response.

87. Had to make an important decision with limited facts.

88. Were forced to make an unpopular decision.

89. Had to implement an unpopular decision.

90. Were tolerant of an opinion that

was radically divergent from
your own.

91. Were disappointed in your
behavior.

92. Used your political savvy to push
through a program you really
believed in.

93. Had to deal with an irate
customer.

94. Delegated a project effectively.

95. Surmounted a major obstacle.

96. Set your sights too high.

97. Set your sights too low.

98. Prioritized the elements of a complicated project.

99. Lost (or won) an important contract or sale.

100. Hired (or fired) the wrong person.

Best Questions

1.   Tell me about yourself using only one-word adjectives.

2.   What have been the biggest success and biggest mistake of your career?

3.   What was the most useful criticism you ever received?

4.   Describe the best person you ever worked for or who worked for you.

5.   If your last boss were able to wave a magic wand over your head, what aspect of your performance would he or she fine-tune?

6.   If you had the opportunity to do the last ten years of your career over again, what would you do differently?

Best Questions

7. Describe the most difficult decision you ever had to make. Reflecting back, was your decision the best possible choice you could have made? Why or why not?

8. If I were to speak with your current supervisor, what would he or she say are your current strengths and weaknesses?

9. Take as a given that you got this job, and that you have been doing it for three to six months, but things are just not working out. We are sitting here discussing the situation. What do you think you would say about what went wrong?

10. When you've had a really good day at work and you go home and kick back and you feel satisfied, what was it about that day that made you feel really good? When you have had a really bad day at work and you go home and feel upset, what was it about that day that made you feel really upset?

Q.   *"Please tell me about yourself using only one-word adjectives."*

A.   The first question cuts through the creative writing of the résumé and the stage acting of the interview (none of which is bad, merely obfuscating). The order of the adjectives is as much of a window as the adjectives themselves. The candidate will hit a very detectable pause after he or she has offered up the pertinent ones (usually three to six) and then it's time to move on to a discussion of "why" to each one of those adjectives. Follow-up questions might include: Have you always been that way? For example (name one of the adjectives), have you always been like that? If not, what caused you to change? What are the highs and lows that each of those adjectives have brought you?

Gordon Housworth

Managing Principal
Intellectual Capital Group
Franklin, Michigan

CHAPTER 4

WHAT DO YOU WANT FROM THIS JOB?

25 Questions to Determine Motivation

The questions in this chapter relate to what motivates a candidate. Every candidate is motivated by money—that is a given—although in the puzzling choreography of job interviews, money matters are relegated to the end of the interview (see Chapter 9).

However, some candidates are clearly motivated by values other than money: technical challenge, the opportunity to travel, the opportunity to learn new skills, the chance to work with a particular individual, etc. It is always useful for the interviewer to determine just what motivates a candidate, especially given the fact that a number of candidates are unclear about their motivations themselves.

1. What motivates you to put forth your greatest effort?

2. Describe your "dream" job.

3. What is the most important feature to you in a job?

4. Please rank the following from most important to least: job duties, hours, distance from work, pay, work environment.

5. What has been your greatest accomplishment in a work environment and why?

6. How important are external deadlines in motivating you?

7. How do you feel about your present workload?

8. Give me an example of a situation where you had to go above and beyond the call of duty to get something done.

9. What do you do when things are slow at work?

10. What have you learned from your mistakes?

11. What two or three accomplishments have given you the most satisfaction? Why?

12. How can we best reward you for doing a good job?

13. Why do you think you'll be successful in this job?

14. What makes you proud of your work?

15. Tell me about a time when you went "out on a limb" in a job.

16. How do you like to be managed?

17. What kind of supervisor is likely to get the best performance out of you?

18. How important is it for you to learn new skills?

19. What new skills would you like to learn?

20. Do you consider yourself successful?

21. What are the most important rewards you expect out of your career?

22. What is more important to you: the salary or the challenge?

23. What do you think determines a person's success in a firm?

24. Tell me about a project that really got you excited.

25. Do you generally clear your desk at the end of each day?

Tired: Where do you expect to be in five years?

These days, no one can think that far ahead.

Wired: Six months from now, when you look back at

your performance here, what specifically do you want to have accomplished?

Q. *"I'd like to hear about what you want to be when you grow up."*

A. Yes, I like to ask it just this way, whether I'm talking to a mid-level manager or a senior officer. Without exception, candidates seem to get a chuckle out of it. In answering this very open-ended question, I have learned that not everyone talks about their professional careers. Some people talk about traditional career matters, but others talk about personal, family, and quality of life issues.

Tony Rucci

Executive VP of Administration
Sears Roebuck & Company
Hoffman Estates, Illinois

CHAPTER 5

SO, TELL ME ABOUT YOURSELF
25 Background Questions

The way we see the world—the way we deal with the major and minor challenges of life, the way we communicate, the way we learn, and the way we play—remains consistent throughout our lives.

Everyone has a preferred way of doing things. Some people are more intuitive, others more deductive. The realization that people bring different modes of problem solving to bear on corporate challenges has been a positive influence on organizations which often boasted having bosses with the attitude "It's my way or the highway!"

In recent years, much attention has been focused on behavioral "types." Some companies actually ask final candidates to take such personality tests as the Myers-Briggs Type Inventory, or the Kolbe Conative Index to get a sense of their styles or approaches to teamwork and problem solving. These firms report that these tests help companies avoid the stress and frustration that grow out of the misplaced expectations that result when mismatched contributors are placed on a team.

A battery of personality tests can reveal a candidate's problem-solving style. But tests are expensive and time-consuming, and some applicants resist them. The following questions are designed to offer a more limited set of insights into how a candidate approaches interpersonal communications, risk management, creativity, and working with others. In other words, they let an applicant showcase what he or she means by "doing what comes naturally."

1. What distinguishes a great employee from a good one?

2. Do you set performance standards for yourself?

3. How do you cope with stress on the job?

4. How do you know if you're doing a good job?

5. What do you need from your supervisor?

6. How will you communicate your frustration when those needs go unmet?

7. Would you rather formulate a plan or carry it out?

8. What was the last business or management book you read and what did you learn?

9. Where or to whom do you turn for help? What resources do you look for in completing a task?

10. What strategies do you use when you have a great deal of work to accomplish and not much time to do it?

11. Describe a time when you used your intuition to good result in support of a project.

12. Where would you like to go from here in your career, and how do you plan to accomplish your goals?

13. In what ways do you and your supervisor think alike?

14. How did you handle a relationship important to your organization when it was threatened?

15. How do you react when someone criticizes you?

16. What do you do when you have to make an important decision?

17. What does the word "success" mean to you?

18. What does the word "failure" mean to you?

19. How do you go about making important decisions?

20. What have you learned about working well under pressure?

21. Do you anticipate problems or react to them?

22. Would you describe yourself as a risk taker or someone who plays it safe?

23. What problems do you have getting along with others?

24.   Rate yourself on a scale of one to ten.

25.   What is your greatest strength?

Tired: Tell me about yourself.

This so-called "killer" question suffers from two defects. First, every candidate has rehearsed an answer to this predictable question. If you want a rehearsed answer, ask away. Second, asked at the beginning of the interview, the question gives the candidate too much power in determining the content of the interview.

Wired: Tell me about yourself using words of one syllable.

CHAPTER 6

ALL FOR ONE AND ONE FOR ALL
30 Teamwork Questions

The ability to work in teams is emerging as the fundamental criterion of success in today's flattened, cross-functional, virtual organizations. The questions in this chapter help the interviewer elicit information about the applicant's attitude toward teamwork and his or her experience working with others in teams.

1. Define cooperation.

2. What kinds of people do you prefer to work with?

3. What kinds of people do you find it difficult to work with?

4. Tell me about a time when you said no to someone who asked you to drop everything to help them out.

5. Tell me about a time when a team fell apart. Why did it happen and what did you learn?

6. Tell me about a job or project where you had to gather information from many different sources and then synthesize the information in support of a business challenge.

7. How do you schedule and commit to quiet time?

8. How do you operate as a team player?

9. How do you deal with people with different backgrounds and value systems different from your own?

10. Do you prefer working with others or working alone?

11. What good or bad work habits did you pick up from your first job?

12. How do you know when a team has met its objectives?

13. Describe your approach to evaluating risk.

14. What is one thing a teammate can say to you that is guaranteed to make you lose confidence in him or her?

15. How do you get along with superiors?

16. How do you get along with coworkers?

17. How do you get along with people you've supervised?

18. What are your team-player qualities? Please be specific.

19. What have you learned about guarding against "groupthink"?

20. Have you developed any special techniques for brainstorming?

21. Are you able to predict a people's behavior based on your reading of them?

22. Tell me about a specific accomplishment you have achieved as a participant in a team.

23. Tell me about a time when your team made emotional decisions about the project. What happened and how did you handle it?

24. Tell me about an occasion when the team objected to your ideas. What did you do to persuade the team of your point of view?

25. As a team leader, how much tolerance do you have for mistakes or false steps? In other words, if a team member wanted to do something in a way you were convinced was a mistake, how would you weigh the team member's learning experience against protecting the project?

26. Have you ever been in a team where people overrule you or won't let you get a word in edgewise? How do you handle it?

27. In any team, there will always be a range of aptitudes. Not only is the spread of talents obvious, but team members are in remarkable agreement about the distribution.

Put any ten people in a room and they will sort themselves out from top to bottom in short order. My question is, do you believe it is useful to the organization to formally rank team members?

28. As a member of a team, how do you see your role?

29. As a member of a team, how do you handle a team member who is not pulling his or her weight?

30. Tell me about a time when you had to confront a team member.

Q. *"If your last boss were able to wave a magic wand over your head, what aspect of your performance would he or she fine-tune?"*

A. My interviewing style has been described as passing out rope.

Alan M. Forker

Senior Vice President
CareerLab
Denver, Colorado

CHAPTER 7

CAN YOU TAKE THE HEAT?
25 Stress Questions

At first blush, these difficult questions may seem to fraternize with the stress interview. This is not so. The stress interview is a discredited technique. The object of such an interview is to see how the applicant reacts to being placed in a highly stressed and uncomfortable position. Stress interviews generally consist of long periods of silence, an argumentative interviewer, provocative challenges, and other techniques.

There's a difference between a stress interview and asking difficult questions. Most interviews include a certain amount of stress by their very nature. The questions in this chapter are stressful only to the same degree that reality presents managers with stressful situations they are expected to address. These questions are designed to be very difficult and thought-provoking, much like the problems applicants will encounter on the job. They are most appropriate for senior managers who will function in fast-moving environments characterized by high stakes and high risks.

Remember that there are no right or wrong answers to these questions. Interviewers should resist the temptation to favor applicants whose responses happen to be aligned with their own. Rather, they should pay attention to the quality of the applicants' logic and their communications skills. Were they thoughtful or did they barge into an answer? How organized were their responses? After considering their initial response, did they ever change their minds?

1. What cherished management belief have you had to give up in order to get where you are?

2. Tell me about a time when your employer was not happy with your job performance.

3. Who is the toughest employer you ever had and why?

4. Have you ever had to work with a manager who was unfair to you, or was just plain hard to work with? Please give details.

5. What's more important to you, truth or comfort?

6. At what time is it better to ask for forgiveness than to ask for permission?

7. Have you learned more from your mistakes or your successes?

8. Is honesty *always* the best policy?

9. How has your tolerance for accepting mistakes from your subordinates changed over the years?

10. You want to go swimming in a pool. The water is a little colder than comfortable. Are you the type of person who jumps in or do you wade in?

11. Where do you think the power comes from in your organization? Why?

12. How will you handle the least interesting or least pleasant tasks of this job?

13. What have you heard about the company or department that you don't like?

14. If you were going to be fired, how would you like your supervisor to handle it?

15. On what occasions are you tempted to lie?

16. How have you been an agent for change in your current (or last) position?

17. Your supervisor tells you to do something in a manner you are convinced is dead wrong. What would you do?

18. What would you do if everyone in your department called in sick?

19. Say your supervisor left an assignment for you in your In-box, then left town for a week. You can't reach him and you don't fully understand the assignment. What do you do?

20. There are two applicants for one job. They have identical qualifications in every respect. How do you decide?

21. What do you want to hear first, the good news or the bad news?

22. What are some of the things your supervisor did that you disliked?

23. If you were on a magazine cover, what would the magazine be and what would the headline say?

24. What kinds of things do you worry about?

25. Finish this sentence, "I know I am taking a risk when ..."

Top Ten

Toughest Questions

Top Ten

Toughest Questions

1. What cherished management belief have you had to give up in order to get where you are?

2. What's more important to you, truth or comfort?

3. Have you learned more from your mistakes or your successes?

4. Is honesty *always* the best policy?

5. How has your tolerance for accepting mistakes from your subordinates changed over the years?

Top Ten

Toughest Questions

6. Where do you think the power comes from in your organization? Why?

7. On what occasions are you tempted to lie?

8. Is the customer *always* right?

9. If you could organize the world in one of three ways—no scarcity, no problems, or no rules—how would you do it?

10. Should all business relationships have fixed terms, that is, expiration dates?

Q. *"When you've had a really* good *day at work and you go home and kick back and you feel satisfied, what was it about that day that made you feel really good?"*

Q. *"When you have had a really* bad *day at work and you go home and feel upset, what was it about that day that made you feel really upset?"*

A. In answer to the first question, technical people will offer as a reason for a really good day the solution of a really juicy technical problem. A bad day for them is often when they had to deal with other people. This is important information, because the jobs I'm staffing are people jobs. These are very effective questions in distinguishing candidates who may be great technicians but who would be uncomfortable dealing with people to the extent the job requires.

Elizabeth St. J. Loker

Vice President, Systems & Engineering
The Washington Post Company
Washington, D.C

CHAPTER

8

CAN YOU THINK ON YOUR FEET?
25 Thoughtful Questions

Today's volatile business environment requires that knowledge workers be able to think clearly, synthesize information rapidly, and take responsibility for making difficult decisions. Moreover, many jobs demand that company representatives be able to articulate those decisions to important constituencies, such as shareholders, the media, or government regulators. When such skills are essential elements of a position, the following questions may be helpful to interviewers as they attempt to assess the ability of candidates to think on their feet.

These questions are designed to test a candidate's ability to think clearly, to make decisions quickly, and to communicate their responses. They are especially useful for assessing applicants who will be expected to articulate or explain corporate policy, to be a spokesperson for the company, or to respond to crises.

1. What was the last product or service you saw that took your breath away?

2. What's the most significant compliment anyone has ever paid you?

3. How has your perspective of quality evolved over your career?

4. Is the customer always right?

5. How would you finish this sentence: "Most people are basically...?"

6. If you could organize the world in one of three ways—no scarcity, no problems, or no rules—how would you do it?

7. Who has been a major influence in your life?

8. How has your tolerance for accepting mistakes from your subordinates changed over the years?

9. Have you learned more from your mistakes or your successes?

10. What's the unwritten contract between you and the people who report to you?

11. How have you benefited from your disappointments?

12. Can you suggest three reasons why manhole covers are round?

13.   We are sending you on an assignment in Santa Barbara, California. You have an unlimited expense account. What kind of car are you going to rent?

14.   Are you the type of person who likes to make lists or strike items off lists?

15.   What would you do if your boss gave you a direct order to pursue a policy that you disagreed with?

16.   What if the board of directors was reviewing a policy that would make such an activity improper but hadn't ratified it yet?

17.   What would you do if you saw a peer taking office supplies home?

18. Describe a situation where your work or an idea was criticized.

19. The business world is full of euphemisms. What's your current favorite?

20. Should all business relationships have fixed terms, that is, expiration dates?

21. Is there anything positive to be said about conventional wisdom?

22. What did you accomplish at work the day before yesterday—in detail?

23. What's the difference between a manager and a leader?

24. What is your philosophy of mentoring?

25. This is a role-play question. You are a consultant hired to assess me and the organization. Based on your observations at this interview, describe my operating style and those of all the other people you have met. Finally, tell me how I could improve the organization.

Tired: What is your greatest drawback?

Most candidates will reply with a variant of "Well, I probably work way too hard and put in way too many hours!"

Wired: What is the most useful criticism you ever received?

CHAPTER
9

MONEY MATTERS
25 Questions about Money

It's a paradox. The first concern that virtually all employers have is "How much money will I have to pay?" Candidates want to know "How much money will I get?" Therefore, one would think that a job interview would address the money issue straightaway. This is not the case because no one likes to talk about money. There is a great deal of pretense around money that relegates it to the end of the interview. This may be inefficient, but that's the way it is.

The result is that every employment guide recommends that candidates avoid discussing salary requirements before securing real interest from the employer. The universal rule that job candidates learn is that they should do two things before even talking about money. First, they should persuade the interviewer that they are the best person for the job. Second, job candidates must get the interviewer to tell them the salary range of the position before they reveal how much they are making or how much they expect to earn. Experienced job candidates will offer all kinds of diversions designed to distract interviewers from talking about their current earning situation or expectations.

At the same time, however, the interviewer is keenly interested in getting a sense of the applicant's monetary requirements. Interviewers may be within their rights to insist on direct answers to straight questions such as "What are you earning now?" or "What's the minimum salary you will accept?" but framing the questions in such a naked fashion can blow a blast of cold air on an otherwise amiable interview. The questions in this chapter offer the interviewer an alternative means of getting the same information. Some questions related to noncash compensation are also included.

1. Can you review your salary history for me?

2. What salary, excluding benefits, are you making now?

3. How can we best reward you?

4. What kind of salary reviews or progress would you expect in this company?

5. In your professional opinion, how much do you think a job like this should pay?

6. What do you think you're worth?

7. Why do you think you're worth that?

8. How do you think your compensation should be determined?

9. What value can you add to our organization?

10. How much money do you want to be making five years from now?

11. How much did you make on your last job?

12. What sort of salary are you looking for?

13. Would you be willing to work for less?

14. What was the last raise you got? Were you satisfied?

15. How would you justify a raise to your current supervisor?

16. The salary you're asking for is near the top of the range for this job. Why should we pay you this much?

17. How would you feel if a person reporting to you made more money than you?

18. Is money the most important aspect of the job for you?

19. What do you think of a process where subordinates have a say in the compensation of their supervisor?

20. What salary do you expect to make in this position? What do you base that figure on?

21. Have you ever worked on commission? Tell me about it.

22. Why aren't you making more money at this point in your career?

23. On what criteria do you believe you should be evaluated and compensated?

24. How important are stock options or deferred payment plans to you?

25. What noncash aspects of your compensation are important to you?

CHAPTER 10

ASSESSING SPECIFIC SKILL SETS

251 Questions for Specific Disciplines

ENTRY LEVEL

1. What extracurricular activities were you involved in? What made you choose those? Which of them did you most enjoy, and why?

2. What led you to select your major? Your minor?

3. Which of your courses did you like the least?

4. Was there a course you found particularly challenging?

5. If you were to start college over again tomorrow, what are the courses you would take? Why?

6. In college, how did you go about influencing someone to accept your ideas?

7. Based on what you know of the job market, which of your courses were the most useful? The least?

8. What advice would you give to a college student intending to go into your field?

9. What are your most memorable experiences from college?

10. What did you learn from your internships or work study experiences?

11. Why don't I see internships or work-study experiences on your résumé?

12. In what courses did you get your worst grades? Why? How do you think that will affect your performance on the job?

13. Why did you decide to go to college?

14. How was your college education funded?

15. What percentage of your college did you pay for and what sort of jobs did you have while you were in school?

16. Tell me a little about some of your extracurricular activities that would assist you in this job.

17. Why are you working in a field other than the one in which you have a degree?

18. What have you done to stay current in your field?

19. Are you satisfied with the grades you received in school?

20. Do you think your grades accurately reflect your ability?

21. Have you ever received a grade lower than you expected? If so, what did you do about it?

22. Have you ever been put on the spot by a professor or adviser when you felt unsure of yourself? How did you handle it?

23. What competitive activities have you participated in? What did you learn from participation in competitive activities?

24. Has competition had any positive or negative impact on your accomplishments? How?

25. What's one management lesson you learned in college?

26. Why do you want to get into this field?

27. I see that you do not have very much organizational work experience. What qualities do you have that especially qualify you for this position?

28. Your résumé does not list any job experience in the past few years. Why not?

29. Why would you want to leave an established career at your present employer for an essentially entry-level position?

30. What specifically have you done that shows initiative?

31. What are the reasons for your success?

32. What are some of your pet peeves?

33. Which of your skills can stand improvement at this time?

34. Who (or what) has been a major influence in your life?

35. Are you a self-starter? Can you give me an example?

36. Can you think of a challenge you faced? How did you deal with it?

ADMINISTRATION

37. Under what conditions have you been most successful?

38. Tell me about a time when you had to pull a team together quickly.

39. How, specifically, do you contribute toward an environment of teamwork?

40. What can you do to build teamwork here?

41. What has been the employee turnover in your department over the past two years?

42. How do you define employee morale?

43. What programs have you implemented to build morale among those reporting to you?

44. How do you keep your staff informed of new developments and organizational decisions?

45. Describe the relationship you feel should exist between a supervisor and those reporting to him or her.

46. Have you ever had to make an unpopular management decision? Tell me about one of those decisions and how you handled it.

47. How do you go about assigning and scheduling projects and assignments?

48. Describe your leadership style for me.

49. How do you measure your success as a leader?

50. How do you determine which individuals need additional training?

51. What training have you offered other people? How do you measure its impact?

52. If you are hired for this job, how will you approach the first thirty days?

53. Do you believe in the value of strategic planning?

54. What is the most intellectually challenging thing you are looking for in a job and why?

55. How did you prepare for this interview?

56. What do you do when you know you're right and others disagree with you?

57. Finish this sentence: "Successful managers should ..."

58. What are the advantages of diversity in the workplace?

59. What does the term "time compression" mean to you?

60. What does the term "total quality management" mean to you?

61. Other than money (which is a given), what do you believe motivates people?

62. Can you give me three elements of your personal code of ethics for the workplace?

63. What experiences do you have in your background that show you are capable of creative risk taking?

64. What were your most memorable accomplishments in your last job?

65. Did you inaugurate any new policies (or systems) in any of the positions you've held?

66. What is the most difficult thing you ever tackled? How did you approach the problem?

67. What work is the most monotonous for you?

68. What does the term "global competition" mean to you?

69. Tell me what you think would be some good approaches to developing overseas markets during the next three years, especially considering the state of the dollar in today's international markets.

BUDGETARY/FISCAL MANAGEMENT

70. Describe the most significant internal control weakness you ever identified and what you did to remedy it. What were the results?

71. Describe the most significant accounting operations reengineering project you have led. What were the results?

72. Do you perform employee salary reviews? If you do, what is your approach?

73. Tell me how you go about creating an annual budget.

74. What problems do you have in staying within your budget?

75. Distinguish between planning for the short, mid, and long term.

76. How do you quantify the results of your activities as a manager?

77. Have you ever completed a formal Return-on-investment calculation on a strategic investment? Please provide details.

78. Which spreadsheet programs do you prefer to work with?

79. How do you deal with unanticipated expenses? Can you give an example?

80. How do you evaluate the budget in your present position?

81. Tell me about a time when you underestimated a budget and had to ask for additional moneys.

82. Did you ever have to restructure your budget in the middle of the fiscal period? What approach did you take?

83. How would you create a budget in the position for which you are applying?

84. If we adopt a 401(k) plan, how often would you perform discrimination tests?

GENERAL MANAGEMENT/ SUPERVISION

85. What's the hardest thing about being a leader?

86. Are you a mentor to anyone? Who? What is your philosophy of mentoring?

87. What does the word "success" mean to you?

88. What does the word "failure" mean to you?

89. Describe a problem that you solved using employee involvement.

90. Tell me about the most difficult employee situation you ever had to handle. What did you do and what was the result?

91. Tell me about an employee who became more successful as a result of your management.

92. Describe your system for controlling errors in your own work and the work of your staff.

93. Which management gurus do you find most interesting?

94. What do you want to be doing five years from now?

95. What are your most important long-term goals?

96. Describe the people that you hired on your last job. Were they successful? How long did they stay with the company?

97. What has been your experience with major expansion or reduction of force?

98. How many immediate subordinates have you selected in the past two years? How did you go about it? Any surprises or disappointments?

99. How many immediate subordinates have you removed from their jobs in the last few years?

100. How do you feel your subordinates would describe you as a delegator?

101. Some managers keep a very close check on their organizations. Others use a loose rein. What level of control do you prefer? How has it changed in the last few years?

102. What have been the most important surprises you have noticed from things getting out of control?

103. Let's talk about standards of performance. How would you describe your own standards? What would your subordinates say? What would your boss say?

104. Sometimes it is necessary to issue an edict to an individual or the entire staff. Do you have any examples of recent edicts you have issued?

105. What specific behaviors do you think contribute to your effectiveness as a supervisor?

106. From an opposite viewpoint, what behaviors do you think might interfere with your effectiveness as a supervisor?

107.   In what respects do you feel you have improved most as a supervisor during the last few years?

108.   Some managers are quite deliberate about such things as communications, development, and motivation. Do you have examples of how you addressed these areas?

109.   How would you characterize your relationships with your last three supervisors? Any patterns?

110.   Some managers are short-fused and impatient in their reactions. How would you describe your own patience?

111. Most of us can look back upon a new idea, a new project, or an innovation we feel proud of having introduced. Would you describe one or two such innovations you are particularly proud of?

112. What are the legitimate uses for office gossip or the rumor mill?

113. How would you handle a subordinate who deliberately went about a task in a way that contradicted your instructions yet was wildly successful?

114. Your boss is going on vacation for a month, and although it isn't in your job description to do so, she asks you to work for another manager in her absence. What would you say and do?

115. Are you prepared to fill in for someone who has different, even lower-level, responsibilities?

116. Describe a time when you unfairly got caught up in office politics.

SALES & MARKETING/SALES MANAGEMENT

Tired: Will you eventually want your boss's job?

What do you expect them to say? Who really wants that job, anyway?

Wired: How important is it for you to move up in management?

_____

117. Can you sell me on our product (or service)?

118. What strategies do you employ for finding common ground with your customers?

119. Can you give an example of how you are able to be positive about a product even when discussing a negative?

120. Have you found it helpful to take notes when talking to a customer? How?

121. If I were a prospect, what clues about me does this office give?

122. What strategies do you use to repeat the customer's key concepts back to him or her during a sales pitch?

123. How do you turn an occasional buyer into a regular buyer?

124. Have you ever taken over an existing territory or desk? What was the volume when you started? What was it when you left?

125. What have you learned about using sales incentives to promote sales?

126. What strategies do you use to plant questions in your customer's mind?

127. When is it appropriate to ask a prospect, "How much do you want to spend?"

128. Tell me about a time you adjusted your approach to a prospect based on their body language.

129. Tell me about a time when you followed up with a reluctant prospect and still failed to get the order.

130. Talk about a time when you overcame your own mental block or prejudices to make a sale.

131. Can you talk about a sales incentive program that motivated you?

132. Who are the motivation gurus you find most interesting?

133. When was the last time you sent a thank-you note to a customer?

134. How do you try to show each customer that he or she is important?

135. This job requires a large amount of travel. Do you think you have the ability and willingness to keep up?

136. When you cold-call a prospect, what obstacles do you expect the clerical staff to put in your way?

137. When you telephone a prospect, what strategies do you use to get past the secretary or receptionist?

138. Where do you find your telephone leads?

139. What do you despise about telephone sales?

140. How do you qualify a prospect?

141. How do you overcome the difficult periods that face everyone in sales?

142. How long does it usually take you from initial contact to sales closing?

143. What is your ratio of initial contacts to actual sales presentations?

144. What percentage of your sales calls result in sales?

145. How would you go about identifying customers in a new market?

146. What do you think about prospecting for customers or developing new markets in cyberspace?

147. Tell me about a time when you almost lost a sale and worked hard to get it back.

148. What are the five most common objections you face and how do you deal with them?

149. What was the most surprising objection you have ever received, and how did you handle it?

CUSTOMER SERVICE

150. What's your definition of customer service?

151. Can you tell me about a time you took the steps necessary to resolve a problem although it wasn't technically your responsibility?

152. Name one way in which you have provided extraordinarily good service—above the call of duty—to a customer or client.

153. Describe a situation where you had to go an extra mile for a customer.

154. Give me an example of a time when you went out of your way to meet an agreement.

155. In your current job, who are your customers?

156. If you had a customer who was complaining about poor service, how would you handle it?

157. At your last job, how often did you take a survey of customer satisfaction?

158. Tell me about your worst customer service dilemma and how you overcame it.

159. What strategies have you learned to encourage customers to pay on time?

160. Can you tell me about a difficult collection problem and how you dealt with it?

161. What strategies have you evolved to listen to emotional customers without getting hooked?

162. Speak about the customer's "personal zone" and how you use it.

163. How do you deal with customers who think they are right even when they are wrong?

164. What is the customer service attitude at your present organization?

165. How have you handled customers who take advantage of sales support staff?

166. What is the most significant improvement in customer service that you have achieved in the last year?

167. What's one thing we at this company could do to make our customers even more satisfied with us?

INTERPERSONAL COMMUNICATIONS

168. What experience have you had in making oral presentations? How do you rate your skills in this area?

169. At what times do you have trouble communicating with people?

170. How would you compare your oral skills to your written skills?

171. When you are assigned to work with new people, how do you go about getting to know them, how they work, and what their strengths and weaknesses are?

172. Tell me about a work situation that required excellent communication skills.

173. Can you recall a time when you persuaded someone who initially disagreed with you of the correctness of your position?

174. How often do you communicate with the person who receives the output of your work?

175. What's one thing that should never be communicated in a memo or e-mail?

PROJECT MANAGEMENT/ DECISION MAKING

176. What are some examples of important types of decisions or recommendations you are called upon to make?

177. Would you describe how you went about making these types of decisions or recommendations? With whom did you consult?

178. Tell me what you have learned about reducing employee turnover.

179. What organizations do you see as this company's chief competition? Can you compare and contrast the organizations?

180. What do you do to make the people around you feel important, appreciated, and respected?

181. How do you prioritize your time?

182. What decisions are easiest for you to make and which ones are more difficult?

183. Most of us can think of an important decision which we would make quite differently if we made it again. Any examples from your own experience?

184. Most of us become more astute decision makers as the base of our experience broadens. In what respects do you feel you have improved as a decision maker?

185. Describe a situation that required you to use fact-finding skills.

186. Tell me about a complex problem you had to deal with.

187. Tell me about a time when you failed to reach a goal.

188. How many projects can you handle at a time?

189. Think of a crisis situation where things got out of control. Why did it happen and what was your role in the chain of events?

190. Give me an example of a time when management had to change a plan or approach to which you were committed. How did you feel and how did you explain the change to your team?

191. Do you use an activity chart to track the flow of the activities necessary to reach your goals?

192. What project management methodologies have you found most effective?

193. I'm interested in how you do your planning. What planning processes have you found useful, and how do you go about implementing them?

194. In what ways have you improved in your capacity for planning?

195. Tell me about a job or project where you had to gather information from many different sources and then create something with the information.

196. What do you do when there is a decision to be made and no procedure exists?

197. What have you learned about using deadlines to motivate people or teams?

198. Tell me about a time when, rather than following instructions, you went about a task in your own way. What happened? Would you do it the same way if you had to do the task over again?

199. Can you think about a specific situation where you prevented a problem before it occurred?

HIRING/DISCIPLINE/ TERMINATION MANAGEMENT

200. What do you do to welcome and orient new hires into your department or team?

201. If you were hiring someone for the job you are interviewing for, what three qualities would you look for?

202. What questions would you ask, or what techniques would you use, to establish that the person was willing to do the job?

203. How many people have you hired in the past two years? Into what positions?

204. Do you have a favorite interviewing question?

205. Tell me about how you would budget for recruiting.

206. What has your experience been with retaining recruitment firms?

207. How do you handle personnel evaluations?

208. What's the first thing you look for on a résumé or application?

209. How do you go about checking references?

210. Tell me about your biggest hiring success.

211. Tell me about your biggest hiring mistake.

212. How could we improve the hiring process we are using to select a person for this position?

213. To what do you attribute turnover?

214. Is turnover always detrimental?

215. What programs have you found to be successful in retaining employees?

216. What is your concept of discipline?

217. What are the typical problems and grievances that your staff bring to you?

218. How do you handle them?

219. How do you maintain discipline within your department or team?

220. Tell me about a time when you had to discipline a subordinate.

221. What was the most common cause of termination at your last organization?

222. Have you thought about violence in the workplace? What strategies have you evolved to address this problem?

INFORMATION TECHNOLOGY MANAGEMENT

223. How do you keep abreast of new developments in information technology (IT)?

224. Describe a situation in which you were able to enhance the usefulness of information in an existing mainframe system and increase your employer's productivity.

225. How has your conception of information systems quality evolved over the years?

226. Describe successful strategies for software testing that you have employed.

227. What metrics can be used to measure user satisfaction with IT?

228. What strategies do you recommend for organizations facing the year 2000 problem?

229. How would you reinvent our business from an IT perspective if you had a blank piece of paper and no resource constraints?

230. We know that fourth generation languages (4GLs) have many benefits. Which of these benefits do you find most compelling? Why?

231. How can you tell a good program from a bad one?

232. *InfoWorld Magazine* recently suggested that client/server computing is dead. Do you agree, and if so, what killed it?

233. What is the future of the mainframe in a world of distributed desktops?

234. Describe the most significant business process reengineering project you have led. What were the results?

235. Distinguish between the Internet and the Intranet.

236. What is the chief benefit of an object-oriented application development paradigm?

237. Describe the central attributes of the object paradigm. How does encapsulation or polymorphism contribute to the technology's effectiveness?

238. Why has computer-assisted software engineering (CASE), a technology which offered so much promise, generally not met the high expectations set for it?

239. Which Rapid Application Development (RAD) methodology do you find most interesting or effective?

240. Describe a data migration project you led. What were the results?

241. I see that you have listed Java, Pascal, COBOL, and C++ as the programming languages with which you're familiar. Would you take a moment to rank them according to your skill level?

242. What structured programming methodologies have you found most effective?

243. Please describe the most difficult task you ever had to perform using tool X, and describe how you managed to accomplish it.

244. Which computer trade shows do you regularly attend and what do you get from them?

245. Have you ever presented at an industry trade show or seminar?

246. Have you published anything on IT?

247. Describe your participation on an IT steering committee. What was the challenge? What was your role? And what was the outcome?

248. With respect to the IT steering committee, what technology did you choose? Why? How did it work out?

249. Do you have any experience with Rapid Application Development? Tell me about an application developed using this approach.

250. Have you participated in the design and deployment of a Web site?

251.   Do you have an e-mail address or a personal Web site?

Q.   *"If you had the opportunity to do the last ten years of your career over again, what would you do differently?"*

A.   With this question, I look for a degree of thoughtfulness. Has the applicant brought a level of consciousness to the question? The question also provides valuable clues as to how settled the applicant is in his or her chosen career. I look, most of all, for evidence of joyfulness and satisfaction.

Fran Sincere

Director of Human Resources
Kaiser Permanante
Denver, Colorado

Q. *"Describe the most difficult decision you ever had to make in your professional career. Reflecting back, was your decision the best possible choice you could have made? Why or why not?"*

A. All of us have made difficult decisions in our professional careers. If we look back on these decisions, chances are pretty good that we could have made different decisions from time to time. In this question, I am looking for a response to see if candidates are really honest with themselves and with me. A sound response goes something like this: "At this particular point in my career, I did this and, looking back on the decision, I could have made a better choice and here is why I think so." I am impressed with candidates who are at least introspective enough about their own choices and their own decision making to admit that they occasionally could have made a better choice and, looking back, have learned from the mistakes.

David Swan
Vice President
Leprino Foods
Denver, Coloado

CHAPTER
11

CLOSING THE INTERVIEW

15 Questions to Draw the Interview to a Close

How you close the interview is just as important as how you open it. When the time available for the interview is ending or you have all the information you think you need to make a decision, the interview should be closed. Thank the candidate for taking the time to come in. Summarize what you have learned. Finally, give the candidate the opportunity to ask questions. The quality and relevance of the questions asked can be an additional significant clue as to the applicant's qualifications. (See Chapter 13, Now, Do You Have Any Questions?)

The following questions can be used to close the interview.

1. Well, based on what we have discussed, how do you feel about this job?

2. Do you have any questions?

3. Is there anything else I should know about you?

4. I've interviewed several very good candidates, and I will admit that you are one of them. What single message would you like me to remember that will convince me that *you* are the one we should hire?"

5. How do you feel you performed during this interview?

6. What have you been able to learn about our firm and our senior management?

7. What implications have you drawn from the information?

8. When can you start?

9. Are you willing to travel?

10. Are you willing to relocate?

11. May I contact your present employer and references?

12. Is there anything you'd like to know about the job that would help you to do it better than anyone else could?

13. If there were one reason why we should select you over the other applicants, what would that be?

14. Our time is about up. Is there a final point you would like to make?

15. Do you want this job? [One hopes the answer is positive.] Then why, through our entire discussion, have you not asked for it?

———————

Tired: How long would you stay with our company?

No one can predict job continuity. Not the candidate. Not the interviewer. Why not acknowledge reality?

Wired: When will you know it's time to leave this organization?

———————

CHAPTER 12

DO YOU HAVE A PROBLEM WITH THAT?

25 Questions to Help Identify Applicants Who May Be Disgruntled or Prone to Violence

Workplaces everywhere have become scenes of violence. The National Institute for Occupational Safety and Health reports that in 1994, 1,071 Americans were murdered at work and 160,000 were physically assaulted. The average cost to employers of a single episode of workplace violence can amount to $250,000 in lost work and legal expenses, according to the National Safe Workplace Institute.

Psychologists believe that most persons prone to violence fit into a certain personality profile. The traits in this profile include lack of self-esteem, poor impulse control, and a sense of victimization. This chapter lists a number of questions which, when combined with a scrupulous preemployment screening process, may be helpful in identifying candidates with these problems. Of course, not all candidates who have some or even all of these traits act out violently. There is no formula. It's the interviewer's job to make an assessment based on the candidate's total presentation.

Most of the questions in this chapter focus on how candidates perceive they were victimized by their former employer. The common thread among all incidents of workplace violence is a feeling of victimization: that an employee was treated unfairly by his or her colleagues, supervisors, or both. These candidates harbor feelings of real or perceived unjust treatment or lack of respect from their coworkers. What's more, if you ask the questions in a relaxed, interested manner, without a hint of judgment, many applicants will be unable to resist answering. That's because most troubled applicants feel that if they just tell the interviewer the facts as the applicants perceive them, the interviewer will accept that they were victims of injustice. They will discuss all the injustices they had to suffer at their former place of employment and how they hope they will not have the same situation at their new job. The interviewer has to assess such revelations on a case-by-case basis.

Prescreening, combined with reference checks and personality tests, is a company's best strategy for minimizing workplace violence. An experienced interviewer can use the interview process to identify temperamental candidates: those who exhibit evidence of short fuses or thin skins. If candidates badmouth their last employer for making changes or criticizing them, there is little sense in offering them a job because making changes and criticism are par for the course in any job.

There are no guarantees in the hiring process. If there were, there would be no need for this book or, in fact, 90 percent of the Human Resources industry. The details—legal and otherwise—of screening candidates for a safe workplace is beyond the scope of this book. Nevertheless, as part of a well-considered screening program, the following interview questions can help weed out potentially violent candidates.

1. How would you finish this sentence: "Most people are basically...?"

2. Tell me about a time when your employer was not happy with your job performance.

3. Have you ever had to work with a manager who was unfair to you, or was just plain hard to work with?

4. How would you define a difficult manager?

5. Have you ever been in a dispute with a supervisor? What was it about and how was it resolved?

6. Can we check your references?

7. What kind of references do you think your previous employer will give you? Why?

8. How do you deal with coworkers or supervisors who do not show you proper respect?

9. What causes you to lose your temper?

10. How do you handle rejection?

11. What are some of your pet peeves?

12. Which of your skills can stand improvement at this time?

13. What problems do you have getting along with others?

14. What are some of the things your supervisor did that you disliked?

15. Were you ever dismissed from a job for a reason that seemed unjustified?

16. What kinds of things do you worry about?

17. What are some of the things that bother you?

18. If I were to call your supervisor today, how would he or she describe you?

19. Can you identify some weaknesses for which you need to compensate?

20. Can you name three new skills, techniques, or methodologies you learned in the past 12 months?

21. What do you do when your boss loads you down with a great deal of work and not enough time to do it in?

22. What do you do when there is a decision to be made and no procedure exists?

23. Are you generally lucky or unlucky?

24. What aspect of your performance in your last job were you the most proud of?

25. If you were going to be fired, how would you like your supervisor to handle it?

Q. *"Take as a given that you got this job and you have been doing it for three to six months but things are just not working out. We are sitting here discussing the situation. What do you think you would say about what went wrong?"*

A. I'm looking for evidence that the candidate has some insight into their limitations and accepts responsibility for them. This is not an acceptable response: "There is no possibility that things will not work out." This is acceptable: "Sometimes I'm so anxious to get things done that I move too fast, I miss details, and I fail to close the loop with people. That sometimes gets me into trouble." This answer tells me that I may need to help this applicant to maintain focus and stay organized.

Tom Morgan

Vice President
Pencom Systems, Inc.
Technical Recruiting Group
Chicago, Illinois

CHAPTER
13

NOW, DO YOU HAVE ANY QUESTIONS?

25 Questions the Interviewer Should Expect to Be Asked

If a candidate has not done a diligent investigation of your firm and its key staff, the candidate either does not know that the information exists or has no real interest or commitment. In either case, the applicant's failure to ask suitable questions might cause you to significantly lower your estimation of the applicant.

Be prepared for questions about benefits. According to a survey of Human Resources executives, interviewees seem to have benefits on their minds more than anything else when it's their turn to ask questions. Thirty-six percent of applicants asked about benefits, according to the 1996 survey by Robert Half International, Inc., based in Menlo Park, California.

Over 150 Human Resources executives replied to the following question: "Other than base salary and bonuses, what do most applicants ask about during job interviews today?" After questions about benefits came questions about corporate culture (34%), job security (15%), and equity options (11%).

A well-prepared candidate always has a number of questions ready to ask. If the candidate you have just interviewed is sharp, be ready for some of these questions or their variants:

1. By what criteria will you select the person for this job?

2. Why is the position open?

3. What happened to the last person holding this position?

4. What duties and responsibilities does this job entail?

5. Where does this position fit into the organization?

6. What kind of person are you looking for?

7. When was the last person promoted?

8. What are the ideal experience and skill set for this position?

9. To whom would I report?

10. What problems might I expect to encounter on this job?

11. What is the normal salary range for this job?

12. Tell me about promotions and advancement in this company.

13. Why are you not filling this position from within?

14. What are your expectations of the person hired for this job?

15. What are the three most significant things that need to be accomplished in this position in the first year and what are the major hurdles?

16. What is the work environment like day to day?

17. How many people will I supervise? What are their backgrounds?

18. Who has the final say in this hiring decision?

19. Is there anything else I should know about this company?

20. Are there any aspects of my background or skills that you would like to hear more about?

21. Is there a job description? May I see it?

22. How much freedom would I have to determine my work objectives and deadlines?

23. What kind of support does this position receive in terms of people and resources?

24. How would my performance be measured and how is successful performance usually rewarded?

25. Can you describe your organizational culture?

A. Top 10 Off-the-Wall Questions

1. What do you want to be when you grow up?

2. Give me three reasons why manhole covers are round.

3. If you were on a magazine cover, what would the magazine be and what would the headline say?

4. When is it better to ask for forgiveness than to ask for permission?

5. You want to go swimming in a pool. The water is a little colder than comfortable. Are you the type of person who jumps in or do you wade in?

6. There are two applicants for one job. They have identical qualifications in every respect. How do you decide?

7. What do you want to hear first, the good news or the bad news?

8. Are you the type of person who likes to make lists or strike items off lists?

9. The business world is full of euphemisms. What's your current favorite?

10. This is a role-play question. You are a consultant hired to assess me and the organization. Based on your observations at this interview, describe my operating style and those of all the other people you have met. Finally, tell me how I could improve the organization.

B. Top 10 Questions for Entry-Level Candidates

1. Based on what you know of the job market, which of your courses are directly transferable to this job?

2. Do you feel your grades are an accurate reflection of your work? If not, why not?

3. In college, how did you go about influencing someone to accept your ideas?

4. Have you ever been put on the spot by a professor or adviser when you felt unsure of yourself? How did you handle it?

5. What competitive activities have you participated in? What did you learn from participation in competitive activities?

6. What's one management lesson you learned in college?

7. Why do you want to get into this field?

8. What are your career goals and how do you plan to achieve them?

9. I see that you do not have very much organizational work experience. What qualities do you have that especially qualify you for this position?

10. What specifically have you done that shows initiative?

C. 25 Additional Questions Interviewers Should Expect to Be Asked

1. Would you mind if I took notes during the interview?

2. What are your plans for company expansion?

3. How many employees would I supervise?

4. Can you tell me why this position is available? What became of the person formerly in this position?

5. What management style is most prevalent here?

6. How many employees have held this position in the last three years?

7. Is this a newly created position?

8. What have you liked most about working for this company?

9. How much supervision will I get as a new employee?

10. Can you briefly tell me about the people I will be working with most closely?

11. Does this company typically have a reactive or proactive strategy for dealing with problems?

12. Let's say that I excel in this position. Where would I go from there?

13. What are the company's plans for the next five years?

14. How would you describe the corporate culture at this location?

15. Describe the performance evaluation procedures you use.

16. What tasks will occupy a majority of my time?

17. What challenges do you think I will face in this position?

18. Describe for me the staff I will supervise.

19. Could you show me a formal job description?

20. Does this position involve any travel?

21. What will be my first assignment?

22. Does this company typically promote from within?

23. How does this position/department fit into the organizational structure?

24. You said I could expect to make more money down the road. When will I get a review and what exactly will I need to do to be successful?

25. When can I expect to hear from you about the next stage in the interviewing process?

D. 25 Acceptable Personal Questions

The bottom line is this: All interview questions should be job-related.

If you're not sure about a question, apply this test: *Does the question go to business necessity? Does the question relate to this individual candidate's ability to perform the tasks for which he or she is being considered?*

Contrary to popular belief, federal employment laws do not expressly proscribe interviewers from asking questions about an applicant's gender, color, religion, or national origin. On the other hand, state laws are more specific, often publishing for employers' guidance lists of "acceptable" and "unacceptable" questions. In any case, it makes sense for a number of reasons to avoid any questions that have no legitimate direct link to the performance of the job in question.

The Equal Employment Opportunity Commission (EEOC) enforces laws against job discrimination, including Title VII of the Civil Rights Act of 1964, the Pregnancy Discrimination Act, the Age Discrimination in Employment Act, the Equal Pay Act, and the Americans with Disabilities Act. It publishes the *Uniform Guidelines for Employee Selection Procedures*. Over 30 states also have nondiscrimination laws. The laws governing the hiring process are complex and outside the purview of this book. It is the responsibility of anyone in a hiring position to understand these laws and how they affect the firm's employment procedures and practices.

The basic point is that while the EEOC and the various state agencies are not particularly interested in the questions asked by an employer, they are vitally concerned about how the employer uses the *answers* to the questions. Asking dubious questions leaves companies vulnerable to discrimination lawsuits. The very act of asking such questions sets up an implication that the company will use the answers discriminatorily. It is for this reason that the Human

Resources departments of many companies enforce rules against company interviewers asking certain questions.

Acceptable: What is your name?

Unacceptable: What is your maiden name?

Acceptable: What is the address of your residence?

Unacceptable: Do you own or rent your home?

Acceptable: Are you over 18 years of age?

Unacceptable: Are you over 40 years old?

Unacceptable: How old are you?

Unacceptable: How many years has it been since you graduated from college?

Unacceptable: Would you have any difficulty working for a boss who is younger than you?

Acceptable:	Can you, if offered a job, submit verification of your legal right to work in the United States?
Unacceptable:	Where were you born?
Unacceptable:	Are you a U.S. citizen?
Acceptable:	What languages can you speak or write?
Unacceptable:	That's an interesting accent. What country do you come from?
Unacceptable:	What was your first language?
Acceptable:	Describe the role of your family in your career.
Unacceptable:	What does your spouse think about your career?
Unacceptable:	Are you married, divorced, separated, or single?
Acceptable:	Were you ever convicted of a crime?

Unacceptable: Were you ever arrested?

Acceptable: Are you capable of performing the essential responsibilities of the job?

Unacceptable: Do you have any physical disabilities?

Unacceptable: Have you ever received workers' compensation?

Unacceptable: Do you have problems with alcohol or drugs?

Unacceptable: Do you have HIV or AIDS?

Acceptable: What are you currently earning?

Unacceptable: What is your economic situation or status?

Acceptable: Statement by employer of regular days, hours, or shifts to be worked.

Unacceptable: Does your religion prevent you from working weekends or holidays?

These questions are usually acceptable.

1. Tell me about yourself.

2. What was your favorite subject in school?

3. Did you have a favorite teacher?

4. How do you get along with people?

5. What kind of person do you get along with best?

6. What magazines do you read regularly?

7. Describe your character.

8. What's the last book you've read?

9. What's the last movie you saw?

10. What do you do to stay in shape?

11. Do you have any physical problems that may limit your ability to perform this job?

12. What do you like to do when you're not at work?

13. What hobbies do you have that might help you perform in this position?

14. Are you satisfied?

15. What makes you angry?

16. How would your coworkers describe you?

17. How do you generally handle conflict?

18. How do you behave when you're having problems with a coworker?

19. Describe your best friend and what he or she does for a living.

20. In what ways are you similar or dissimilar to your best friend?

21. Do you like to travel?

22. What are your hobbies?

23. Are you an overachiever or an underachiever? Explain.

24. Are you an introvert or an extrovert? Explain.

25. Do you set goals for yourself?

E. 75 Unacceptable Personal Questions
Questions Dealing with Age

1.   How old are you?

2.   When were you born?

3.   When were you married?

4.   How old are your children?

5.   When did you graduate from high school?

6.   When did you graduate from college?

Questions Dealing with Disabilities

7.   What health problems do you have?

8.   Do you have any disabilities?

9.   Are you physically fit and strong?

10.   Is your hearing good?

11.   Can you read small print?

12. Do you have any back problems?

13. Have you ever been denied health insurance?

14. When were you hospitalized the last time?

15. Is any member of your family disabled?

16. Do you have AIDS?

17. Have you ever been addicted to drugs?

18. Have you ever filed for workers' compensation?

19. Do you see a physician on a regular basis?

20. When was your last medical checkup?

21. Do you have large prescription drug bills?

Questions Dealing with Ethnic Origin

22. This is a Christian (or Jewish or Muslim) company. Do you think you would be happy working here?

23. What's your nationality?

24. Is that an Irish (or whatever) name?

25. Would working with people of another race be a problem?

26. Where are your parents from?

27. What was your first language?

28. What languages do your parents speak?

29. Are you bilingual?

30. What's the origin of your name?

31. What language do you speak at home?

Questions Dealing with Marital Status

32. Are you married?

33. Are you a family man (or woman)?

34. Do you intend to get married soon?

35. Do you have children?

36. Are you a single parent?

37. What do you do about birth control?

38. What are your long-range plans for family?

39. How many people live in your household?

40. Do you live by yourself?

41. Can you travel?

42. Do you have someone who can take care of a sick child?

Questions Dealing with Religion

43. Is that a Jewish name?

44. Is there any day of the week you're not able to work?

45.   What church are you a member of?

46.   Do you sing in the church choir?

47.   Do your children go to Sunday school?

48.   Can you work on Friday evenings?

49.   What do you do on Sundays?

50.   Are you active in your church?

51.   Are you a member of any religious group?

52.   Are you born-again?

Questions Dealing with Sexual Preference

53.   What's your sexual orientation?

54.   Are you a member of any gay or lesbian groups?

55.   Are you straight?

56.   Do you date members of the opposite or same sex?

Questions Dealing with Personal Finances

57. What's your economic status?

58. What kind of car do you drive?

59. Who paid for your education?

60. Do you have debts?

61. Do you own or rent your home?

62. How much insurance do you have?

63. What is your net worth?

Miscellaneous Unacceptable Personal Questions

64. How much do you weigh?

65. What ties do you have to your community?

66. What social or political organizations do you belong to?

67. How do you contribute to the community?

68. Are you living with anyone?

69. How tall are you?

70. Who did you vote for in the last election?

71. What charities do you support?

72. Have you ever served in the military?

73. Do you think you can work for a younger person?

74. Have you ever been arrested?

75. Do you drink?

About the Author

John Kador has been a computer industry journalist and interviewer for more than 15 years and is renowned for his ability to reveal the human and business aspects of complex computer topics. The author of more than 1,000 published interviews and articles, Kador is in great demand as an observer of the high tech business playing field. He has a number of columns, and contributes to over a dozen leading business publications. Kador earned an undergraduate degree from Duke University and has a Masters degree in Public Relations from The American University. More information is available from Kador's Web site (http://www.otn.com/kador).